DOUBLE DAWG DARE YA!

Growing Up in Cary, North Carolina, in the 1950s and Other Adventures

APRIL RILEY BOLEJACK

WESTBOW·
PRESS
A DIVISION OF THOMAS NELSON
& ZONDERVAN

This book is a work of non-fiction. Unless otherwise noted, the author and the publisher make no explicit guarantees as to the accuracy of the information contained in this book and in some cases, names of people and places have been altered to protect their privacy.

WestBow Press books may be ordered through booksellers or by contacting:

WestBow Press
A Division of Thomas Nelson & Zondervan
1663 Liberty Drive
Bloomington, IN 47403
www.westbowpress.com
1 (866) 928-1240

Because of the dynamic nature of the Internet, any web addresses or links contained in this book may have changed since publication and may no longer be valid. The views expressed in this work are solely those of the author and do not necessarily reflect the views of the publisher, and the publisher hereby disclaims any responsibility for them.

Any people depicted in stock imagery provided by Thinkstock are models, and such images are being used for illustrative purposes only.
Certain stock imagery © Thinkstock.

ISBN: 978-1-4908-7041-0 (sc)
ISBN: 978-1-4908-7040-3 (e)

Library of Congress Control Number: 2015902641

Print information available on the last page.

WestBow Press rev. date: 02/25/2015

CONTENTS

PREFACE

Sixty years ago, Cary, North Carolina was just a sleepy hamlet, a bedroom community for Raleigh, the state capital. There were just a few families who served as the recurring characters in my childhood saga. There were no Italian, Polish, or other exotic last names, just English, Scotch-Irish protestants in our little town. Many more tales will follow, but suffice to say Cary, the fastest growing town in NC, is not the small town of my youth.

I am driven to write this because experience proves that the memory of a person disappears completely in two generations. I want my family to learn what a blessed life I have had, though not without its tribulations. That said, perhaps they will learn through my experiences and how I handled both the good and bad times that everyone is dealt sooner or later if a long life is granted.

I am a baby boomer that is I was born right after WWII. My family moved to Cary, North Carolina when I was ten days old and I lived in the same house there until I was married. They still reside there. What a luxury to be able to live and grow up in the same house, neighborhood, school, and church. Eventually, Cary grew to be a metropolitan area, but there were only 500 families on the tax books when we moved there. What follows is not necessarily in chronological order, but I will try to hit on the important people and events in my growing up.

EARLY YEARS

I was born right after WWII. I was ten days old when we moved into the house where I would live until I was married. It was just a four room, GI Bill bungalow, but what a luxury to be able to live and grow up in the same house, neighborhood, school, and church. What follows in subsequent essays is not necessarily in chronological order, but I will try to hit on the important people and events in my growing up in Cary, North Carolina.

I hope you enjoy traveling this journey with me. I've had a most exquisite party, one filled with love, laughter, good friends, and adventure. The values I learned from my small town youth have served me well all of my life.

Everyone knew everyone else in the Cary of my childhood. I have often joked that we could not get by with much because while we were still planning our adventure, somebody's mother had already called mine and tattled on the whole enterprise. What a safety net that was. Of course, we hated it at the time, but such closeness between neighbors kept us out of a heap of trouble.

Cary was such a safe community. I never heard about any violent crime there during my childhood. In fact, there was more than one occasion when we girls were having a sleep over that we walked downtown in our pajamas after dark to get a soda at the only vending machine.

My siblings and I were allowed to wander all over town to play. Sure, there were certain places we were told not to frequent. But, as long as we were at home in time for meals, we had no restrictions. Today, I will not let my grandchildren out of my sight for fear of who might be lurking to snatch them.

EDUCATION

Cary Elementary School was on the same campus as the historic first public high school in North Carolina. My memory is that the classes held students of all learning abilities. There were no attempts to "track" any students in the education system of the 1950s. The students helped one another by in-class tutoring.

I read everything I could get my hands on. The school library, which served all 12 grades, offered a series of biographies for elementary students. I read all of them. Out of these was birthed a life-long love of history, science, etc. because I got to know the stories and the people who made history.

The subjects were Luther Burbank, Clara Barton, the Founding Fathers, of course, Florence Nightingale, Julia Ward Howe, among others. I also enjoyed the fiction section, I read and reread a book, *Rufus the Red-Tailed Hawk.* I would check it out for the week, turn it in at the end of the week, and check it out again a week later. I loved that book and I think it did much to instill in me a life-long fascination with birds and nature in general. My advanced love of reading did not fit the norm and my teachers and the librarian did not know how to handle me. I am grateful that they were astute enough to give me leeway in what I chose to read.

I was in junior high before we were privy to a reading kit which had its levels color coded. It was presented on cards and of course held only short pieces...no real literature. If I taught reading in the way I believe kids would respond...it would be through REAL literature. There would be no Fry List of words, etc.; maybe kids would stay excited about reading instead of losing their initial eager anticipation. However, then I needed no urging; I had read everything in the elementary section by the time I was in the fifth or sixth grade. So, they turned me loose in the high school section. Under their watchful eyes, I began to discover good literature. In the eighth grade, I stumbled on William Faulkner. First, I read SANCTUARY, then REQUIEM FOR A NUN. I was hooked. I read all that the library offered and wanted more. After all, Yoknapatawpha was not much different from Wake County, NC. Looked at it that way I was reading about people just like those living around me. Faulkner is still one of my favorites today. All the Southern Gothic writers have a style that I wish I could emulate.

During the year of my sixth grade, Mrs. Turner was my language arts teacher. One memory I have is that we worked diligently on diagramming sentences…I loved the process of putting the puzzle together on the frame work. Mrs. Turner was new that year to our school. She had been in some kind of accident or had some type of surgery, for she always wore a small crescent shaped flesh colored bandage under the middle of her misshaped nose. The other kids called her pig nose behind her back, but I respected her too much to participate in their cruelty. She always dressed in a suit and heels…very neat and professional looking. Her demeanor was unquestionably proper. That gave her an air of refinement and credibility which added to the respect she commanded in my eyes. (There is a lesson here for those teaching in our classrooms today.) She was the first teacher to suggest that I had a gift for language and that I should make plans to develop it with some type of post-secondary study. Such a suggestion was foreign to me. I credit her with the idea that I should teach.

I still believe that the ability to use and manipulate language is empowering and education should spend more time empowering students today. I knew and appreciated the value of reading and the importance of quality literature, for I was already reaping the rewards of my skills. Sharing that empowerment has fueled my teaching for the span of my career. Although students frequently voice this question: "Why do we have to read all this junk anyway?" My answer consistently has been: Because literature is all about life and how to live it. This idea and the sharing of it has been my overriding joy for my 27 year career. Our country's founding fathers viewed education as a means of socializing its citizens. All learned and shared a common denominator of knowledge and philosophies. Education today focuses on individualized instruction. This is not a bad idea, but since socialization is part and parcel of the system, aren't we compromising what the stated goals have always been? There is value in learning to function and to be a part of the whole. Our culture is so self-centered and fractured now in the 21st century, it is easy to conclude that education may have, ironically, played a major role in the breakdown of American society.

The teachers I had were all a positive influence on me, with the exception of a second grade disaster. Mrs. Grimes was the third grade teacher. Mrs. Underwood taught the fourth grade. Mrs. Kirby, the fifth. She, I felt, really loved me. My sixth grade teacher was, of course, Mrs. Turner. In the seventh grade we began to rotate classes for different academic subjects.

Mr. Ike Griffin was the seventh grade math teacher. He was easily distracted from the lesson of the day because he had many WWII experiences which we liked to hear and he enjoyed relating. One of my most embarrassing moments was in his class. One day I sneezed and backfired simultaneously. Of course, my classmates heard it and I thought they would never let that one rest.

In the fourth grade, I met Smitty (Linda Smith). She arrived after the beginning of school. Her father had recently left the Armed Services where he had been stationed in Guam. Linda sported an island tan and had pig tails that reached her waist. She was wearing a beige wool jacket that bloomed with embroidered colors which I imagined one would encounter on such an exotic island. She was at once my competition and my everlasting friend. She is still the only person I have ever met who shared the same passion for language and literature. We competed to win the yearly prize for having read the most books. Smitty was all infectious giggles and plots for practical jokes. She was part of every practical joke that I dreamed up…but, sometimes it was a joint effort. One time she wanted to break up the relationship she had with a boy named Fred. She just couldn't face hurting his feelings, so we conjured up this scenario. Trouble was it was probably more hurtful. You be the judge. During this time couples often used one another's lockers between classes. Smitty had to get her stuff out of his locker. The plan was for her to write a note and leave it in the stripped locker. The assigned morning we were at the locker at opening time. Fred usually ran the "almost tardy time" race each morning. Linda had the written note in her notebook…folded in the intricate way that high school "lovers" do.

Goal completed! Now, she was free to look for bigger and better. Around lunch time, there was a buzz in the cafeteria. Fred was flying low…he looked rather pitiful. Word was according to the underground sources…that Smitty's Fred note said, "I Hate You, I Hate You, I Hate You!!! Love, Linda. Painful, pragmatic, and persuasive. It was definitely the MOST effective breakup note I ever helped write. Smitty and I ended our public school careers working on the newspaper at Cary High. I called her Smitty. I was the only one who did so. I called her that until she died suddenly from diabetes. She is part of me. I wrote this about her because I don't know of anyone else who offered a memorial to her, one of the funniest, smartest, and most intelligent girls I have ever known. Lord, I do miss her giggle.

THE WORDSMITH

She came for a short space;
We were both so young,
Not knowing life's not hours,
Or days that can be strung.
But, all our days are numbered
In space and time and plan,
Given more to pleasure
And less to diagram.
We were everlasting friends;
Our days were innocence,
Leisure time spent planning
For some distant reminisce.
Now she's gone on before me
To Evian fields serene;
The books there now rewritten,
A most exquisite cuisine.
Books were the catalyst
Words our sacred cause,
Binding us as sisters
That's just the way it was.

©April Bolejack

BACKYARD FUN

Money was tight in the 50s and Dad's salary did not allow for much recreational spending. One of the pleasures we received from my Dad's sacrificial saving of his lunch money was his purchase of an old piper cub. (Mom gave him an allowance of $1/day,) It was a silver plywood model of an airplane cockpit and the front part of the plane, including wings, resting on a metal framework of pipes. A customer sold it to Dad for a fee of $10.00. Daddy borrowed somebody's trailer, hauled it home, and set it up at the edge of the backfield. It brought the Riley kids instant notoriety in the neighborhood. In a nanosecond, we had every kid within a mile back there. We played on it every waking second for a long, long time, years in fact.

One game I recall was Alligator. I think it might be attributed to the movie Peter Pan. The "alligator" stayed on the ground while the victim hung from the bars overhead, trying to get to the other side before the alligator could pull the victim down. If he succeeded, then the loser became the alligator.

Unfortunately Hurricane Hazel hit and changed the games. When Hazel hit about 1954, that plane took its virgin flight over the backfield. Mother recalls seeing it take off over the field, blowing in the winds, bouncing off the trees until it shattered into pieces too small to hold air. We picked up silver plywood scraps for many years. But, truth be told, we enjoyed the frame every bit as much as the "plane" itself. They became monkey bars, a stagecoach, and anything that a child's imagination could conjure. I don't know of many kids who have had a plane in their backyard playground, do you? We enjoyed our popularity!

From a parent's perspective, Mama could watch us out the back window. She did not have to wonder what we were up to doing. The downside was…there were about 25 children in her backyard every day. She never complained, though there had to have been disagreements and skinned knees, but on we played. No wonder we never had a beautiful lawn, but kids don't care about that; I can't remember ever having a pleasant memory about a lush, green lawn, and that is a fact that many adults need to absorb.

Those neighbors who were "child-friendly" had lawns that showed evidence of many feet. Think about it; 25-30 kids playing together every day. Those lawns were packed harder than any clay tennis court.

Keener Street kids played outside in the summer time until it was too dark to see. At the Creel's house, we played hide and seek. Barefooted, we crept around, hiding under bushes and all around the foundation of the house, often stepping on slugs. You remember: The creatures that left a thick gelatinous slime wherever they crawled. If you stepped on one, you had that stuff between your toes until you made a serious effort to get it off. So, when it was time to go home and get in the bathtub, that slug slime was a job to get out from between the toes. It took real elbow grease. It is a memory I can still recall, only now it repulses me. Then, I barely attended to it.

While it was still light, we played a game called Crack the Whip. We formed a line and ran around the yard changing directions rapidly. The person on the back end of the line was jerked around quite violently due to centrifugal force. Once, I was at the end of the line and got "cracked" so hard that I fell, biting my tongue almost in two pieces. The turquoise shirt I had on was instantly soaked in blood. We ran home and Daddy took me to Dr. Yarborough's office. Doc said that he could not stitch the tongue, so I left with the admonition to eat little and drink much for the next few days. We were having one of my favorites, spaghetti, for supper, but I did not feel like eating. Isn't it strange that after all these years, I would remember the accident by the necessary omission of spaghetti? Now, that's the confession of a real foodie.

Mom believed in the healthfulness of outside activities, thus we did not play inside, but stayed outside as much as possible. When it was very hot, we played cards, monopoly, or something else that did not take much effort. Oleta and Sally, two girls arriving later, and I used to rake pine straw up into the shape of rooms and play house for hours.

Other times, I would climb a tree and take a book with me just for some quiet time. I could put a book in the back of my shorts and climb most any tree. Pine trees were a little rough on the legs because of their bark, but that did not stop me. I would stay up a tree for hours, especially if was able to get away from my little sister...more on that later.

Truth is I led a charmed childhood and have only as an adult come to fully appreciate it. Here is a sonnet I wrote about my growing up.

Blithe Childhood

These lines are writ about times idyllic
When throughout the neighborhood all did cleave
To innocent games and friendships they struck,
Accompanied by summer laughter most free.

Playing at dusk long as light would allow.
Chasing and catching in summer's warm night;
We'd yet to taste the bitterness of now,
Young, innocent, we were blithely forthright.

In youth, the meter has yet to unwind
The verse or story that it will yet tell
And the many days it will soon entwine,
Filled with visiting grieves and sorrow's spell.

Unwitting children shouldn't dread the day,
But oblige the innocent heart at play.

ANIMAL TALES: A TALE OF TWO KITTIES

Our parents had great tolerance for the critters we collected through the years. In fact, they provided a few themselves through rescue efforts, etc. We nearly always had a cat or two and our cats were a source of much affection. When I was about ten, we had two black ones at the same time. One, Panther, was a short hair and quite gentle…an excellent mother. The other, YumYum, was a long hair and not particularly friendly. If human, she would have been a case for social services for she was a failure as a mother. YumYum, according to Dad, was a gift from Percy Flowers, an infamous bootlegger, in Raleigh. Dad did Percy's refrigeration work for him. One night he came home from a service call at Percy's with YumYum in tow. In light of her roots, one could understand a lack of social graces. YumYum would birth a litter, and then leave them for Panther to raise. I can still see her with my mind's eye, twitching her tail as she walked off immediately after giving birth in search of more romance.

Another early pet that I remember fondly was our dog, Poopsie. Poopsie was mostly collie, though I do not think she was from elevated stock. Her ancestry left her with the long pointed nose of a collie, but her legs were too short to be anything but friends with the pedigreed stock.

Poopsie was highly intelligent. She treated us as if we were her puppies. I remember that she would pull on our shirts and sit on us if we tried to leave the yard. She also chased any interloper away…. including the occasional car that passed the house. Her tendency to play the chasing game caused Dad much consternation. His remedy was to fill a squirt bottle with ammonia water and get a buddy to drive him past the house. He figured he needed to be in a strange car or Poopsie might not chase the auto. He drove by several times, squirting her in the eyes when she rushed the car. Didn't work! She was smart enough to dodge every car then and every time she chased one. What an athlete!

Poopsie had puppies at least once/year. No one in that era had the money for pet neutering, so we just gave her pups away. One spring she had 14 puppies. There were not teats enough for all of them, so we had to work shifting them in and out of the nursing line so they all got a chance to nurse. We did not lose a single pup. At that time, Cary was still very small, and for years I could drive around town and see her offspring lolling around in the front yards of townsfolk. Even the Police Chief, Midgett had a Poopsie. She was, perhaps, the first "law enforcement dog."

Although they were never considered pets by my family, my snake collection is the only thing my mother hated. Some of the snakes were alive and some were preserved in alcohol. I captured them wherever I could. Once I found a nest of hatching copperheads under our plum tree. I caught several of them and put them in a cage in the utility shed. I went to NH that summer to spend some time with my homesick aunt. I heard that we had no sooner turned the corner than Mom told my brother to go let those snakes loose…every one of them. I never had a chance to gather another group of specimens. Oh, well! Some just have no appreciation for the exotic. My mother's karma was responsible for the payback involving my brother's snakes. It was understandable that they would make a break for freedom in the house several years later. They were never found. It was the stuff of nightmares as far as Mom was concerned, for she was paranoid about those freedom-loving reptiles getting in her bed.

Mom, notwithstanding, I learned a great deal about nature through these adventures…things that were not included in any science curriculum. For instance, most green snakes cannot bite you because their mouths are too small. It wouldn't hurt anyway. Their teeth are very tiny. Some snakes are born from eggs laid and some appear to be born live, but are hatched from internal eggs. Corn snakes look a great deal like copperheads. Toads are born in the water, but leave their aquatic nursery when their legs develop.

Our family loved to laugh and play jokes on one another. Dad played a great joke on Mom once. Dad coiled up a dead corn snake on the back steps so that Mom would be sure to see it on the way to hang the laundry. No one had to hide and watch; we knew exactly when she encountered the snake by the decibel level of her screams. It was a joke I loved to recount…Dad thought so also.

We always had some pet to play with. I am thankful that my parents were so tolerant. My childhood was enriched by animals immeasurably. Today, as a widow, they are my nuclear family, and I can't imagine trying to live alone without my four-legged friends.

Here is a poem that recalls the many hours I spent playing with the ubiquitous litter of kittens born every early spring.

Under the Rosebush

I am in love with the bracing memory of
Sunlight beaming through bare canes
Of the itinerate climbing rose
Under which I hid from the world.
No one discovered my pathway,
Manuvering, first right, then left,
Gingerly, through the thorny mine field,
Thus to bask in solitude and air perfumed
By the fragrance of the blossoms.
The latest litter of kittens served as muses,
Scampering through the protective,
Large canes…Their antics
Vital reflections of my blithe childhood,
While my mother stood on the porch
And called and called my name.
Even now, in the midst of a frenzied day,
I can recall the peace and warmth of my secret place,
Conjuring memories, regenerate and reviving,
For, I am ever in love with the memory of sunbeams.

MISADVENTURES

Growing up in a child-filled neighborhood where the majority was boys created a fierce streak of the competitor in me. When the boys played football, I tackled with the best. Of course, the only playmate on the home front for our first six/seven years was my brother, Daryl. We were extremely close and I thought he was just wonderful, beautiful, and brilliant. Whatever he dreamed up, I was ready to do. We were always together.

That was both blessing and curse, for when we got into trouble, it was often double indemnity. While still preschool age, we played frequently in the field behind our house. There were older boys in the neighborhood who belonged to the Boy Scouts. Once they carelessly left a small hatchet in the field. Of course, we found it. Daryl picked it up and began chopping on a large oak stump. I brushed the resulting chips out of the way. Chop, brush, chop, brush…we were a team. However, with one chop my finger was pinned by the blade cutting my left middle finger off at the first joint with the exception of a small piece of skin, the ring finger was clipped and the little finger had a small cut. I screamed and began to run across the adjoining back yard, holding my left hand and its parts in my right. Finally, I reached the house. Mama recalls that she nearly blacked out. She covered my hand in a towel and walking, most families had just one vehicle and that was Dad's work truck, she carried me the two blocks to Dr. Frank Yarborough's office. He was out on a house call, so we paced the sidewalk outside his office with my hand dripping blood… (Those blood stains were visible for a long time and were a point of pride for me…sort of my *Red Badge of Courage* if you will.) Meanwhile, his nurse/wife called Daddy at work and when he arrived, Mama sat down and fainted dead away. To this day Mama cannot stand the sight of blood. My question is how can a woman birth five children and not expect to encounter a little blood occasionally. Recently, I heard a radio commentator make the remark that surgery for reattaching severed body parts has not been with us for very long. That may be true, but in 1950, Dr. Frank Yarborough sewed my three-year old finger back onto my hand. He told my parents that it might not take, but I was very young and it was worth a try. If it worked, he said, it might take 6 to 12 months to regenerate the bones and nerves. Remember, microsurgery was long into the future…it was Dr. Yarborough's belief that said the nerves and blood vessels might grow back together. Mom and Dad decided to do it and the process was pure agony. The resulting incessant throbbing every night caused me to keep my hand in my mouth to quell the pulsing pain, resulting in many secondary infections. My nails kept falling off from infection and lack of circulation. Finally, they bandaged my hand, placed it in a little sack. Then my arm was placed in a sling, tying it in such a way that it stayed close to my chest. I was really inconvenienced then.

I had many secondary infections...so many that Dr. Yarborough began to doubt that the finger was going to reattach. My great grandmother, Daddy's grandmother, (GarReed, her name is a child's rendition of Grandmother Reed) made a potion of her homemade salve. I don't know what was in it...but it cleared my hand of infection and I began to heal. I remember the odor of that salve, but have no idea what it contained. Sure wish someone knew. It worked miracles.

GarReed was our resident healer I suppose... a major participant in another of my medical incidents: pneumonia. After I got back from a summer camp, where I dove into the water from a platform and had many water fights during the week-long camp, I developed a serious chest infection. I played so hard that I had aspirated some of the lake water which was, I think, the instigator of my illness. Bedridden shortly after arriving home. I don't remember much except that I was deliriously ill. GarReed made another unction; this times a mustard plaster. She and Mama slathered it all over my chest (It burned like fire.) I thought for sure that it would blister me. Then, they piled on all the blankets which they could find, and I began to sweat that infection out. It worked. You see, most people during this time rarely went to the doctor. There just wasn't money for it, nor was it the way of things back then. So, I don't know if I had pneumonia because there was no formal diagnosis. But, I know now how pneumonia feels since I have had it as an adult and my memory tells me that I probably had a dose of it then.

Another back-field adventure involved fire! Mother had her burning barrel in the area which was skirted by a field of broom straw, growing rather thickly. Whenever we could, Daryl and I would play in the fire with sticks. We had to be sneaky to dodge my mother's ever watchful probing eyes. One day we "accidentally" threw a burning stick on the ground in the area sprouting broom straw. Whooosh! In seconds, the field was ablaze. Someone called the Cary Volunteer Fire Department. Red Lights and Sirens...how exciting! We, of course, ran so we wouldn't be blamed. I don't think Mom knew that we did that several times just for the excitement and adrenaline rush. Only after Daryl and I were grown and had left home did we confess to those small acts of arson. Passing time helped us feel it was safe to confess such criminal behavior. Today, we'd probably be arrested, but that was then. In that same field, we fought Indians, rode trees, played baseball, built forts, and caught doodlebugs. There wasn't much we didn't do in that field. It was such a luxury to have that entire vacant lot of about 2 or 3 acres just to hide in and play. Here is a poem about this time in my life; there are many more things to tell.

Double Dawg Dare Ya!

In the springtime of my youth,
There's nothing I wouldn't do;
Double-dawg dare me-that's the cue.
I would, to tell the truth.
Been known to ride a tree;
Pedal my bike as fast as could be,
Down steps, at least thirty-three;
I would, to tell the truth.
Might climb the highest tree
Stop to pick the scab on my knee
Stay there hours just to see.
I would, to tell the truth.
Walk uptown without shoes;
Stub my toe and dab the ooze;
Try my sister first to lose;
I would, to tell the truth.
In third grade, leave school;
Lunch just wasn't cool;
Eat hotdog on the drugstore stool;
I would, to tell the truth.
Play outside in the rain;
Wade with brother in storm drain;
Neighbors said, "...Haven't a grain."
I would, to tell the truth.
Spend hours in the swamp;
Collect frog eggs 'til damp.
Through brackish water tramp;
I would, to tell the truth.
In my autumn, play the sleuth;
Search the Fountain of Youth;
Find its secrets totally mute,
I would, to tell the truth.
But I can live it all again;
Conjure it anew inside my brain;
Find it keeps me more than sane;
I do, to tell the truth.

April Bolejack

NEIGHBORS

Spence and Lela Cotton owned a small plot of land whose boundaries ran perpendicular to our street. Their land adjoined Aunt Mary's and their driveway was just two ruts in the dirt made by their mule and wooden wagon. That wagon was their only mode of transportation. It was a faded buttermilk blue and had yellow, spoked wheels. The wagon seat was a one-person size, so Spence left that for Lela and he sat upon a wooden stool. Their wagon and mule along with the two of them were a fixture in our small community for many years. The clop clop of a horse or mule is something that I miss hearing and I am saddened to realize that most of our youth will never hear that sound as part of their everyday lives. Today, the only sounds when someone passes is the thumping of a ridiculous sound system or the whining speed of a Ninja cycle. Traveling speeds now preclude any interaction between neighbors. We are more concerned with getting there than making small talk with neighbors. In the post war era, Spence and Lela and similar couples in other towns went to town every Saturday visiting to the Piggly Wiggly, a small Southern grocery chain,

While they shopped they hitched their mule to a small tree, providing a spot of shade. The mule was embellished with a flowered hat on to keep the sun out of her eyes and she looked rather festive too. The Saturday shopping was to buy their meager weekly fare. This weekly celebration gave them opportunity to socialize with friends and neighbors. Here's a poem that reminds me of their weekly trips:

Spence and Lela

Now, Spence and Lela Cotton
Lived just round the bend;
We loved to watch their wagon
On days uptown they'd wend.
Every sunny Saturday morn
Spence dressed up their mule;
Lela piled in the wagon;
Spence sat upon a stool.
The mule, she had a milliner;
For style she couldn't be topped.
Her hat had flowers and ribbons,
And the back brim'd been lopped.
Spence had on his overalls;
Flat-ironed to a razor crease.
Lela's do-rag tied so careful;
Its edges stained with grease.
On up Charley Cotton Hill;
They stopped to conversate.**
Check up on the neighbors;
The mule didn't mind the wait.
She clopped straight down Main Street
Without a hurry she'd proceed.
Spence bought groceries at the Piggly,
Picked up just what they'd need.
Then on home they'd go
Taking the trip uphill just so.
Winding back down the road
Carefully traveling to their abode.
Spence and Lela are no more;
Their time has come and gone.
Their souls were of gentle folk,
From an era now gone on.
A simple life was what we shared;
There was no racial strife.
They were just our neighbors,
Spence and Lela, his wife.

©April Bolejack

I would never want to diminish the struggles many endured during this time in the South, but in our little neighborhood we were just neighbors. As you can imagine, I never gave much thought to the richness these neighbors added to my life until I realized that a great change was occurring without my doing anything to instigate it or to stop it. This era just somehow slipped away before I was aware that anything was happening. I assumed that such a time and people would endure, but Spence died first before I married and left Cary. I don't know when Aunt Mary died or the others in that two street section, but Lela met a most tragic death. Lela died on a snowy night after cleaning the local bank, sometime between 1966 and 1969 She had finished and was leaving to go home. She waited on the snowy curb to cross safely, but a car slid on the slick street and plowed right into her, killing her instantly. Aunt Mary, Spence, and Lela took an era with them; they took our lifestyle and those of us who assumed there would be others of their kind to take their places were wrong. There were none who had lived when they had and so we are all poorer for their demise. There have been many changes in Cary, but none has had a greater impact on the flavor of the everyday than the passing of these people.

AUNT MARY

One of the ghoulish delights that my brother and I enjoyed as a benefit from living in our very small town in 1950s NC was the hog-killing days that began as soon as the weather was sufficiently cold. Our neighbors included people who were black and they lived just on the street perpendicular to ours which we called Charley Cotton Hill. Cary was so rural then that we had a chance to see some things we would not have seen in Raleigh, just 8 miles east.

Mama always discouraged us from going to Charlie Cotton Hill where on the first bitter cold morning, the men down there strung their hogs up by the hind feet, put a bullet between their eyes and then slit their throats to drain. They caught the blood in a dishpan and used it I think to make something like blood pudding. It was tantalizingly gory. The folks who lived around Charlie Cotton Hill were a part of our neighborhood and their images are stamped forever in my memory. One endearing member of our neighborhood was a woman we all called A'nt Mary. She wore her hair in white braids and kept cotton stockings on her legs winter and summer. She had some gold teeth and a reputation as a talented prestidigitator. She need only to lift up the front of any expectant mother's maternity smock to pronounce the gender of the baby. I never saw her work outside of the neighborhood, but she was always busy making lye soap to sell to her neighbors. She also cooked greens to sell to those who had no patch in a garden themselves. If a garment was stained so badly as to be ruined, Mom would send it up to Aunt Mary who would boil it in her pot with lye soap and it would emerge spotless. When we could afford it, she would come and iron for my mother. Without her help, my mother would never have seen the bottom of that wicker ironing basket. All day long she'd hum and iron.

After a morning's work, around noon, Aunt Mary and Mom would sit at the kitchen table together, chat about neighborhood news, and eat lunch. In oher parts of the South, the races were segregated. But the two of them ate and chatted at the same table, neighbor to neighbor sharing the latest news because that was what they were, neighbors. She had a son, George, who had a drinking problem. We didn't go around him much, but he sat on the porch regularly watching the world go by. We always had to pass their corner when we walked uptown so we always waved and spoke politely. Here is how I remember both of them.

Ole A'nt Mary (a jump rope chant in voice of young girl)

Ol' A'nt Mary live on Charley Cotton hill;
Ol' brown shack stand up dere still.
Yella eyed Geo'ge dat's huh son's name
Drink, drank, drunk, he in de grave.

Walk down de street on de side of huh shoes;
Boils huh clothes and hum de blues.
Serves huh turnip greens cooked wif fatback;
Thraws huh wash water out de back.

Walk to town ever' Sat'day morn;
Hair braided up en tied in scorn.
Lift up de smocks of de ladies due.
Nevah guesses wrong; she see right through.

Ol' A'nt Mary live on Charley Cotton Hill;
Ol' brown shack stand up dere still.
Greet all de fo'k by dey last name;
Eyes don' hint no resident pain.

Live long enough to see sum gain
Nevah moved off dat land she claim.
Ol' A'nt Mary die on Charley Cotton Hill;
Ol' brown shack stand up dere still.

CHRISTMAS ON KEENER STREET

The street where I grew up did much to populate the post-war generation. All holidays were special and fun because there was always someone who got interesting "loot" from Santa. There was something magical about the way our gifts worked out so that we could all play together. With more than twenty children on our street alone, it was genius that the parents would put their heads together and buy similar presents for the children of Keener Street. In that way, no child was left out because the others received roller skates or bicycles, etc., if one got roller skates, we all got roller skates.

The year the road was paved in the summer, we all received roller skates, the kind with the key that you tightened around the sole of your shoes. It led to great fun, but was disastrous on our foot attire. Without mentioning the skinned knees and elbows, I remember how many of us had a sound that followed us wherever we went. First, the foot hit the pathway, then what followed was a sharp snapping sound from the shoe soles that were torn loose. Foot fall, snap, foot fall snap...you could hear Keener Street kids all over the school that winter and spring. Back then, we didn't have a closet full of shoes; there were Sunday shoes and school shoes and maybe a pair of grungy play shoes. So, when the skates pulled the soles apart from the shoes, we just sucked it up and carried on. The skating was worth it in my opinion. There was to be more than once when I cut cardboard to fit in my shoes so that I didn't have to walk dead on the ground. Maybe that's why I have so many shoes in my closet now, ya think?

The hill at the end of the street where we skated every day seemed so steep and dangerous then. Now, it appears as no more than a slight elevation in the landscape. An adult's perspective is so different from that of a child. We should always remember that. perspective is everything, isn't it?

All the kids on Keener Street entered an informal contest every Christmas to see who would be the first household with the lights on signaling that Christmas day had begun. That family's children had bragging rights the rest of the year. Daryl and I would actually lie in bed and wait until we heard our parents creak down the hall. We'd listen for our parents to emanate the rhythmic breathing that indicates sleep and then we'd spring out of bed and turn on the lights. One of us would look out the window to check if anyone else's lights were already on.

In a year when funds were scarce, my Gandaddy (my mother's father with the name pronounced as spelled without the "r.) found and renovated an old WWII paratrooper's bicycle. It was collapsible and capable of being carried in a knapsack. I wouldn't mind having that bike today; I'm sure it has an impressive value. Dad and Gandaddy restored the bike with new paint, handlebars, etc., but neither he nor Dad noticed that the tires were dry rotted. That Christmas Eve when it was brought in from the cold, the air they had pumped into the tires began to warm and expand. Further complicating the situation was that my Dad's mom was visiting and asleep on the living room couch. The tires expanded until they could hold together no more and BANG!!! They blew. My grandmother sat straight up and grabbed her chest and screamed, I've been shot!" There was no rest in our home that night. She was inconsolable. And, of course, when we caught sight of that bike, nothing could console us until we got the new tires we needed in order to ride it. And, by the way, we won the "first up" bragging rights that year.

Christmas Dreams

When I dream of Christmas,
I never fail to go
Back to the happy times
From childhood long ago.
We'd wake up oh so early
Expecting cold and snow
Always surprised to find
The North wind failed to blow.
Still, that did not stop the party
The turkey or the ham.
It did not stop our family
From gathering to cram.
We'd spend the whole day playing
On bikes and scooters too,
Enjoying one another
While Papa took a snooze.
Mama'd rock the baby;
He was excited too.
It gave her just a moment
To catch her breath anew.
I wish I could go back
To those days of innocence
When all it took to make me smile
Were canes of peppermint.

©April Bolejack

A LITTLE WORK; A LITTLE PLAY

Growing up in a large family (there were five children and always a grandparent or spare uncle added to the mix), money was scarce. Fortunately. I got a job after I reached my teens in order to buy some of the things I thought were crucial. They weren't, but I thought they were. And, I wanted a job that paid more than babysitting. At that time the going rate as a babysitter was 50 cents/hour. When the voice of opportunity called, I snatched the chance to work "putting up" tobacco for the Rigsbee family; they were the parents of the neighbor lady next door. I had never worked on a farm or had much to do with tobacco, but that did not matter. I spent the months of July and August working every day at one of several tobacco barns where they cured their crop. Interestingly enough the pay was $2.00/day. You do the math, butI didn't care; it was hard work; it was fun. The workday started early. By 6:00 AM we were at the barn ready to start. That meant that I had to get myself up around 5:00 AM in order to get some breakfast. We usually ate an egg sandwich in the car on the way to the barn where we would work that day. Those egg sandwiches made with a little butter, salt and pepper and wrapped in waxed paper while still hot, were ambrosia that early. The dew was not off the tobacco when we arrived at the field.

My first day it seemed as if the workers were speaking a foreign language. First, I had to learn the language of the process. The "primers" walked through the field and picked off the largest leaves that were slightly yellow, laying them in a "slide" which was a cart pulled by a mule but without wheels. It was important to keep the leaves without blemish as they brought a higher price at auction, so when they were handled...it was gingerly.

The mule brought the full slide to the barn where its contents were laid upon the bench. About three or four "handers" picked up the leaves by the stalk and handed them two or three at the time to a "looper." A looper wrapped the string around the leaves so that the bunch could be suspended on both sides of a stick while the leaves were held tight. The sticks were then hung on a rack in the barn. Starting at the top of the barn the sticks were hung with enough space between them to ensure good air circulation. When the barn was full, a slow fire was started and the barn was shut up so the leaves could cure. The farmer usually slept at the barn keeping an eye on the contents until the leaves were golden and aromatic. The smell of a freshly cured barn of tobacco was very pleasant; I think it was a process that required several nights, maybe a week.

Our fun started whenever the barn crew got ahead of the field crew and had extra time between slides. We played with tobacco worms so large Hollywood could have made a horror movie about them. Green with black horns and their sides embellished with hairy appendages, they could grow as big as a man's thumb. We threw them at one another and tried to put them in the bundles we handed to the loopers so when the looper grabbed the bundlel, the worm was either squashed or it wiggled around most disgustingly. Other games included hide and seek inside the barn, shooting rats after lunch and going on the rare foray into Carpenter (an even smaller town than Cary) to get snacks for the other laborers. We could do that only if we were working at the barn that was very close to Carpenter's local "country" store. The ultimate reward was to ride the mule to the store. One time I tried to mount the mule for a bareback ride to the store with Earl Jr, the Rigsbee's grandson. The mule got skittish and I ended up back to back on that mule with Earl Jr. The mule did not like that arrangement and I got thrown off and landed on my knees. OUCH!

Eating was all about getting a break. About 10 AM, Mrs. Rigsbee would leave the barn and head to the house to begin cooking lunch. That woman could sure sling some hash. We ate right out of the garden... red, juicy tomatoes, luscious baby butter beans, green beans strung the night before and flavored with a bit of salty ham, okra fried extra crispy, and field peas cooked right out of the field...all served up with a cake of crispy-crusted cornbread (I am salivating even now.) Folks, it just doesn't get any better than that. We had the "eat local" movement then 50 years ago before it was a movement. It was a necessity. For dessert, we would drop a watermelon to crack it open. Even though it was warm from the sun...those were the sweetest watermelons I have ever eaten...they were crisp and sweet with enough juice to make you sticky but we never noticed because we were already coated with sticky tobacco gum that was all over our clothes. After eating the watermelon, the field workers laid down under a tree and napped for about an hour. The kids played until the hottest hours were over and then we picked up the work pace again.

The day was over whenever a field had been primed or picked clean or about 4:00PM. Here is a poem I wrote with those watermelons in mind.

WATERMELON

Honeyed sweet syrup mottling

And trickling down,

Drawing a succulent trail,

Pinking and dripping all

Down my face, sliding

Into a puddle of pure

Melodic satisfaction.

WATERMELON!

©April Bolejack

THANKSGIVING MEMORIES

Most holidays at the Riley house included someone who had no family to celebrate with for whatever reason. My mother took in all kinds of strays. We did not have a lot of extra anything, including food, but Mom always stretched what we had.

Her cousin, Myrtle Upchurch, is one example of a family "stray." I don't know much about Myrtle except that she bore the "Upchurch" name of my ancestors and was a very distant cousin. She had outlived all her close relatives, so we invited her to all of our holiday activities. Myrtle was probably in her eighties and sported short curly white hair on a rather frail frame. She lived in an apartment that could be accessed only by a rickety set of steep wooden stairs. Thinking again, it was ridiculous for her to live up there. Nevertheless, my older brother and I would go and pick her up to join us for the family meal. She always took home the leftovers. I often wondered where she got her other meals. She was a good lesson for us on family loyalties and obligations.

Some of the strays invited to the dining table were boyfriends of mine. My future husband, although we weren't that far into the relationship at the time, came for Thanksgiving dinner one year. He sat down on the couch in the living room and the leg fell off. I don't know which of us was more embarrassed. Later we were called to the table and asked the blessing, then, we passed all the different bowls around and everyone loaded up. Garland, however, was prudent in the amounts he served himself. After some time, he asked for the bowl of mashed potatoes to acquire a second helping. My brother passed him the empty bowl without saying a word. Garland had such a strange look on his face. We all laughed. It didn't take Garland long to learn that at our house, there were no second helpings; one had to get all he wanted on the first pass or lose out...a hard lesson for an only child.

Another time my parents invited the preacher and his wife to Thanksgiving dinner. They had no children...I'm sure the noise level alone was a real shock to their sensitivities. During the meal, the preacher needed another napkin. So, my little sister was given the task of getting more from under the cabinets because she was closest to the kitchen. She came back with a box of "sanitary" napkins. I wanted to melt into the floor. She had the most exquisite ability to humiliate me at that age.

We didn't have an abundance of material blessings, but we had the richest of all bounties...we had a loving family that loved to laugh and that loved one another. Those treasures money could never buy.

GROWING UP BOOMER

In our small town, there were only about 500 families on the tax books my parents say, so we Riley children were not able to go anywhere incognito. We cooked up many adventures, but the safety net of neighbors surrounded us and kept us out of a great deal of trouble. The thing that strikes me as so different now is that then we were safe to walk the three blocks to the uptown area, (it wasn't metro), to spend our weekly allowance or run an errand for Mama. I could not let my grandchildren out of my sight for a single moment. Then, there was the local bank on the corner, the drug store, the hardware store, a movie theater, a 5 & 10¢, service station, a small grocery, and two churches, Baptist and Methodist (If you were not of those persuasions, I guess you were on the "primrose path" so to speak).

A favorite place was The Ken Ben (5 & 10¢); it was the best place to spend a 25 cent allowance on candy. A counter holding candy in glass bins greeted the customer. Such a sight was every child's dream....Upon request, the salesclerk scooped and weighed the buyer's choice into a small white bag. Chocolate covered raisins were my favorite. The coating was real, not waxy and the chocolate melted at first contact with the warmth of my mouth. I would eat them slowly, in singular fashion… never slighting even one.

The hardware store provided unmitigated pleasure for us. They were always willing to give us their empty cardboard shipping cartons for stoves or refrigerators. These were pretty sturdy and after dragging them the three block journey home, would last at least a week as "playground equipment." We camped in them in the summer, used them as "covered wagons," pushed and pulled one another in them, rolled down the hill in Katy Nash's yard and had a great time using them in hide and seek. Cheap entertainment in my opinion.

Sometimes we used our 25 cents to attend a Hop a Long Cassidy matinee on Saturday. The admittance fee covered all day if you so desired. I don't know many who stayed through only one performance. Necco wafers were the treat of choice. A few pennies and you had a long tube of them which when carefully consumed could last through an entire movie. The brown ones, root beer flavored, were my favorites. Another favorite place was Ashworth's Drug Store. Their lunch counter was a dark marble with pull-type soda dispensers, porcelain knobs with brass trim. They made the best cherry and vanilla cokes as well as homemade orangeade sodas, milkshakes, or floats. Homemade egg salad and pimento cheese were also available as cold or grilled sandwiches, but their Hot Dogs were sublime.

Once, when I was only nine years old, I left Cary Elementary School during lunch, walked to the drugstore which was two blocks straight down Academy Street, my school at one end and the drugstore on the opposite end, plopped my little behind on a stool and used my 25 cent lunch money to order a hot dog, bag of chips and a coke. The reason I left the lunch at school escapes me. However, It wasn't long until I saw Mom coming through the back door of the drugstore. Subsequently, I was escorted, protesting profusely back, to school by my mother. She was pretty hot because she had walked the three blocks uptown with my little brother on her hip. I know the lady who ran the soda fountain spilled t he beans reporting me truant with a single phone call. (See, I told you there was no chance of getting by with anything in such a small town.)

We had a longer lunch period in those days. The teachers went to the lounge for about 30 minutes after their classes returned from the cafeteria and the class was put under the watchful eye of a snitch/peer who had been entrusted with the awesome power to "take names." I was often chosen to read something aloud to the class during this time while ice cream was ordered and eaten by those who could afford it. One book I read was *Heidi*. For some reason, I thought that the phrase, "How now, brown cow" was humorous and took the liberty of frequently inserting it into the written text, especially if I had a Fudgescicle in my hand, and then waiting for the desired effect. Upon such illumination, the entire class would collapse into giggles. At this age of knock- knock jokes, that was wielding real power.

About the time I was in the fifth grade, I began to go home for lunch. I loved to do it; the food was much better, and I had a Mama's undivided attention for a few moments. Every trip gave me a chance to catch a frog in the little creek that ran under the road about a block from home. I succeeded most of the time. If it was raining, I simply ran from one front porch to another and still enjoyed my time away from school. Today I would be horrified to see a child running home in the middle of the day. It is not safe. The idyllic childhood which I had is such a blessing. I am sure that if I had not lived it, I would not believe my memories are real. Here is a poem that speaks of much more than I could ever include in this essay.

Boomer

I am a baby boomer
Product of an innocent childhood
When grass was something cut on Saturday
For people in the neighborhood.
Went to the movies for 25 cents;
Saw Flash Gordon, Hop a Long,
Roy and Dale,
Even watched
The Long Ranger
Riding on the trail
Of villains wearing black hats.
Never had to guess at that.
I am a baby boomer;
Grew up in the dark
'bout dangers from strangers
And all such stuff as that.
Went to church each week;
Knew everyone on my street.
Had more mothers than you could count;
Never knew anything about a charge account.
I am a baby boomer;
Spent my time outside each day.
Didn't have TV; had to imagine to play.
Rich was a box of 64
Or a secret decoder ring.
If I had some Ovaltine,
I could do most anything.
I am a baby boomer;
Learned to read with Dick and Jane.
Played marbles every spring.
Collected baseball cards
and later friendship rings.
I am a baby boomer
You will hear me say
I think we had it good
Back in our day!

©April Bolejack

MAMA

I was blessed with a mother who was at once, intelligent, beautiful, and saintly. In fact, I have often referred to her as Saint Frances. In her youth, she was a gypsy-like dark-skinned woman with exotic overtones, black hair and dark brown eyes. Frances J. Riley grew up in Raleigh and according to her grandmother (my Nanny) had the pedigree of several NC governors along with a Native American princess in her lineage. She was an excellent writer and authored several books in the course of her professional career which included being the founding editor of *The Cary News* our town's newspaper.

If one looked for an example of patience, he would not have a hard time coming across my mother as an example. She had five children and for many years we lived in a four-room house with one bathroom. Imagine the chaos on weekday mornings when we were trying to get to school, etc.

But, I get ahead of myself here. I don't know much about my mother's childhood except that she was very close to her Aunt Baba (Mary Moore) and my cousins Carolyn, Sammie Lee, and Kristin. Her younger sister, Ann, used to tell the story of how they would all pick up pecans on the campus of the state hospital for the criminally insane, Dorothea Dix Hospital, and eat the nuts and feed the bitter piths to her. Sorry to say, the three do not deny such a heinous act. According to my aunt, they were always trying to get rid of her because she was so much younger (12 years) than they and "got on their nerves." But the happy times included everyone snow sledding down the rolling hills of that hospital's campus which is still a popular location for such today.

I know that the story of Mom's first date with my father goes like this. One Sunday afternoon, there was a knock on the door and my mother, eating a piece of fried chicken (her favorite food in the whole world) answered with the chicken in her hand. My dad stood there and said, "I've asked everyone else, would you like to go to a movie with me?" My mother accepted his warped invitation. Five children and more than sixty years later, they were still together.

1944's It Couple at Needham Broughton High

He, the handsome Yankee
A new face in the halls.
She was the local Southern girl
Editor, the newspaper called.
Together, "the" couple
That academic year.
Though afar a war brewing
Was being brought to bear.
He, a dashing dancer;
She, the writer with lair.
He, coal black hair
She, exotic beauty fair.
1944, the playing field
Converted and in part
Changed to a theater
Touting foreign ramparts.
Fast forward 64 years.
Now, five children later
Both finished careers
The rest they craved now granted.
What's left for the future,
For "the couple" of the year?
Every battle's been fought;
Their future is not here!

©April Bolejack

Mama has never seemed to want much for herself. I remember one time when Dad bought her a new outfit, dress and shoes. It was a very big occasion and much was made of the event so it had to be unusual. She wore that outfit so proudly and I thought she was beautiful in it.

Mama has a well-honed sense of humor and the ability to laugh at herself. Having such was purely survival instinct for she had to be a magician to make Dad's salary feed all of us.

She had to be able to multi-task in order to keep ahead of the game. Once she was talking on the telephone and washing dishes at the same time. The phone slid into the sink of sudsy water and Mama just kept talking and waited until she finished her conversation before she fished the phone out of the soapy water. The phone did not work after that and had to be replaced.

It takes a brave soul to confess such as story as this next one, but we have all laughed over it many times. Mama says when my brother, Daryl, was born, she was only nineteen and full of fear and trepidation that she would make a mistake. She had no experience with babies, so every little bit of direction or advice she followed to the letter. She mentioned to Daryl's doctor of the difficulties that her baby had with bowel movements. The doctor instructed her to do the following: sterilize her finger and insert it into the rectum to stretch it. She thought that meant sterilizing as she did his bottles, so she held her finger in boiling water as long as she could stand the pain and then followed the doctor's instructions. After boiling all ten fingers, she called him and queried, "Now, what do I do, I am all out of fingers? These are too sore to use again." Now, that's naïve.

I guess her sense of humor was inherited from her father, Gandaddy. That's the name my brother and I gave him. Here's an example of his wit. It was encumbered to him that he give us a goat. I don't know why, but he did. We named it AEthelbert…and we did not know that the name was the same as the first Anglo-Saxon king of England. Just another example of the strange language my brother and I used with one another. Anyway, with the goat came a cart which the goat was supposed to pull, taking us wherever we wanted to go. Suffice to say, no one consulted the goat, and mama pulled the whole contraption what few feet we ever traveled in tandem. I just remember AEthelbert eating the clothes on the clothesline and the cellophane wrappers off of Dad's cigarettes. We eventually donated her to a herd kept by the agriculture students at NC State. I don't think Mama shed a single tear when that goodbye was spoken.

We children always loved to hear Mama and her sister, Aunt Ann, get together because it inevitably involved something funny happening. One holiday season they discovered a craft project that they felt deserved trying. It consisted of collecting tin cans and using metal cutters to cut the cans into strips and twisting with pliers the side cuts into curls. A vicious task to say the least. They were then spray painted gold and attached to one another for a sunburst type wall decoration. It looked just as what it was...cheap and lethal. Not too many years ago, we found one Mama had made in the attic and wrapped it up and gave it to her for Christmas. That little jewel gave regifting a new dimension. We all laughed at the memories it presented.

Suffice to say, my Mama, as true with many others, sacrificed a great deal of herself, her goals, and her dreams to be a matchless example of modern motherhood. Here is a tribute to her:

Mother

When the streetlights appeared
And the dust on the road
Had settled at day's end,
I listened for your call.

Your voice traveling
Across green lawns
Of neighbors,
Calling us home to
Bath time and bed.

Summer feet and
Sweaty bodies led us
To bathe; we dared
Not lay down until
Scrubbing off the day.
You patiently helped
Us don our PJs
And settled us with
A story before sleep,
Of Bambi or the Ugly Duckling.
Sometimes the soft
Strains of radio adventures
Lulled us to relax,
Lone Ranger or
The Green Hornet
Filling our sleepy thoughts.
How I long to hear you again
Whenever the streetlights
Are aglow and I am
Tired from the day's "play."
I listen for you, Mother, and
Sometimes I hear your call.

© April Bolejack

DAD

My dad, Robert Riley, is a charmer, especially with the ladies, so it is natural that I was a Daddy's girl. I think he is one of the hardest working people that I know. Although, he cannot do what he used to do, he knows how to teach someone else what to do. He could put together, take apart, and generally fix anything that needed fixing. He loves old movies and there were many times when we used the free passes he got from his customers who owned local drive-in and theaters, (he worked on heating and cooling units,) to attend some corny, old B movie. Mama would pop a grocery bag full of popcorn, fill the thermos full of Kool Aid and off we'd go lawn chairs in the back of his pickup to the local drive-in theater. We saw some real good movies and some strikingly bad ones. One memorable double feature was *Attack of the Killer Shrews* (since named worse movie ever made) and *Giant Gila Monster*. If we weren't appropriately scared, Dad would sneak up on us sitting in our chairs placed close to his truck for protection, then yell "BOO!!!" It would cause us to scream giving all the reinforcement for the next time he wanted to play the same trick…we fell for it every time. Now, he likes the watch the old Westerns and can name every actor playing a part. Along with his love of old movies, Daddy loves good music. He was quite the smooth dancer in his day, and I know that he has never liked the new rock and roll noise as he calls it.

Dad had a rough childhood and tried to see that ours was better and he succeeded. I don't think as a child that I appreciated the sacrifices he made, such as, saving his lunch money all week so that we could buy ice cream on Sunday nights. He is an excellent cook. I loved it when he cooked Sunday lunch or got a wild hair and tried to make fudge. He would get so upset when the fudge failed to set up, but it was my favorite when I had to eat it with a spoon. Yum!!!

Daddy always had to do the "medical/first aid" stuff because Mama couldn't stand the sight of blood. One summer my brother and I both had impetigo and staph boils at the same time. His job was to lance those boils every night. What a disgusting job after working all day.

Daddy worked with Gandaddy in an air conditioning/heating sales and service. It was hot work in the summer and freezing cold in the winter. He rarely ate a meal at night that he did not receive a service call. Some customers were not as quick to pay their bills as they were to request service. I remember one delicatessen owner who was slow to pay. The business rigged up a system where the customer had to put a quarter in a box on the meat cooler for it to run. It didn't take long to get their money. Pretty ingenious, wouldn't you say?

Sometimes I would go out with Daddy after supper. Mama was too tired and we would go to a movie and get pie at his favorite, Blue Tower Restaurant. Daddy wouldn't eat at many restaurants; he had access to the kitchens and knew which ones were clean.

Of the two of them, Daddy was the disciplinarian. Mama was often too busy with one of the younger children to do more than say, "Just wait 'til your father gets home." Sometimes we could get him tickled and he would just give us a good talking to, but when the twinkle left his eye, we'd better be looking for a book, towel…just anything to slip into our pants. Of course, he always found the protection. After dishing the discipline, Dad came back about 2 or 3 minutes later to give us a reassuring hug so that we knew we were still loved. Undoubtedly, we deserved whatever punishment we received.

I really don't know how either Mom or Dad kept their sanity with five children in a small house. It made us close; it could have made us dangerous.

As I got older, I found that Daddy was a sucker for a "snow job." If Mama said, "Go ask your father," I'd just get in his lap and say…"oh, Daddy, please let me go." He was a weak man when it came to that technique and I loved to watch him disintegrate into a gelatinous mass.

Over the years, I have come to appreciate the sacrifices that Mom and Dad both made for us. I don't suppose that they thought much about it, but as a parent I sure have. Great role models… these two were for their relationship and the kind of parents we wanted to be.

OUR FAMILY

Our family was large. Five children, various grandmothers, a great grandmother and pets too numerous and transitory to count made up our colony We moved into a very small four-room house in the "new" section of Cary, NC when I was 10 days of age. There were only two children in the family at that time. The rest of the brood came later...it was to be six years before my sister arrived. Mom and Dad had my older brother during the war when they were so young, 19 years for both. I arrived when they were at a more experienced age ...21. We had to grow up together.

Daryl, my older brother, was strikingly handsome. We shared the nursery and were as close as any siblings could be, actually inventing a rather complicated secret language, using it to pass secrets to one another. If you saw one of us, you saw the other. As a first born, he was naturally dominate in many areas, but I did not care for I was born with a ready playmate. We did everything with one another. I can remember sharing the nursery while I was still in my crib. We both bucked the bed. At least that was how we referred to the rhythmic rocking back and forth after we got on all fours. I once woke to find my bed in the hall. I have always been blessed with a remarkable memory, in fact, my earliest memory is of Mama moving my crib to the wall beside the door next to the light switch. I discovered how to turn the light on and off and you know the rest. I remember getting my butt swatted and told to lie down and go to sleep. I must have been about a year old.

Daryl and I had many games we played after we were in bed. We played "bird nest" which involved wadding up our bed linens around us (I know Mama loved this game) and chirping like baby birds. We also rode bed bikes. That involved lying on our backs, putting the soles of our feet together and pumping them as if we were pushing bike pedals. We could get rather noisy with that one and insight a reaction from Mama. We tried every trick to get up and see what Mom and Dad were doing. One thing we were allowed to do was to watch *I Love Lucy*.

Nap times were mandatory, and we were keenly aware of the amount of time we had to stay in bed. There was a plane that flew over daily at the same time. (I think it must have been around 3 PM.) And that was my cue. If I heard that plane, I knew if I asked Mama, I would be allowed to get up. Mama often surprised us with the Cookie Fairy. The fairy would visit while we were napping. We awoke to the lovely smell of freshly baked cookies. Now, there just isn't anything better than warm cookies and cold milk to wake you up. Unfortunately, no one appears to realize that I still need this. But, I passed the tradition on to my children and I sometimes have the Cookie Fairy visit the grandchildren when they are here. I have just begun to tell you about the magical childhood with which I was blessed. But suffice to say, of our little family of four which was going to grow by three more, no one was more important than my brother. Here is a poem which I read at his funeral. God, I still miss him. He was in many ways my hero.

My Brother

Who shared my room
While we were tykes
And with but feet
We rode **bed bikes?
My brother.

Who played with me
And made the rules
And showed me secrets
'bout using tools?
My brother.

Who helped to set
The field afire
And watched to see
Our mom perspire?
My brother.

Who showed me
How to ride my bike
Down thirty steps
And stay upright?
My brother.

Who marched with me
Through thick and thin
And never squealed
Or showed chagrin?
My brother.

Who is so close
It can be said
That we were one
'Til we each wed?
My brother.

©April Bolejack

ARRIVAL OF MARY-MICHAEL

I think it was 1953 when the world as my brother and I had known it ended. Someone else with whom we were to share the limelight showed up. She arrived on a sunny day in May, my grandmother's birthday, and was just so cute. I remember being allowed to hold her that day. I did not realize how important she would be in my adult life, but what child ever realizes that?

From the beginning, it was obvious that she was very bright and wanted to be a part of everything. She was my shadow and at times that was stifling, though I am sure that my mother was appreciative of the distraction. She was very attached to me because I could not stand to hear her cry, so if she woke in the night and began to cry, I got her out of her crib and put her in bed with me. Soon, she had to sleep with me every night. In fact, we slept together in an old iron bed until the night I left for my honeymoon.

Along with the big sister/ little sister part of our relationship, there was the normal rivalry. I tormented her, but she just kept coming back for more. One story was that I told her my real name was Abel, not April, and that I had been killed by Cain. That always upset her, though I don't know why because logically if I were dead, I would not have been there. She always cried anyway and that was the goal. I spent no small amount of time tricking and teasing her. One always reliable torture was the "Test of Real Beauty." I administered this almost daily while in the bathtub together. We would both rub the bar of soap between our hands, then I would tell her to wash her hands under the water. She would rub hers together, but I would just pretend to do so. The test was if after taking our hands out of the water we could still create a lather, it proved that we had real beauty. Of course, she could not, because she had actually rubbed her soap off, but I could…that was living proof that I was more beautiful than her…It always elicited an appropriate response.

Later, she would pay me back tenfold when we no longer took baths together. The closet in our room shared a wall with the bathroom. The pipes to the tub ran up the back of the closet. There was a small opening where the faucet joined the pipes. It was not uncommon for me to be lounging in the hot tub water, feel that paranoid sensation of being watched, open my eyes and find her green eyeball filling that hole, spying on my nakedness. I couldn't get away from her even when I was in the tub for crying out loud. I would scream and tell Mama, but Mary-Michael always denied it. I resorted to hanging a washcloth over the hole.

As she got older, I got more inventive in my quest to shake this shadow. Often I would grab a book, put it in the back of my shorts and climb the sweet gum tree outside the back door. She would come outside calling for me. If she happened to walk under that tree, I would drop a sweet gum bomb on her head. She never figured out what was happening, but there was no end to the satisfaction I received from those secret sorties.

Another place that I hid from her was under a rosebush that grew up the side of the house. It had massive canes and had grown rather hollow underneath. Perhaps the warmth of the south side of the house contributed to its size. I would grab the latest kittens and a book, then hide under that rosebush for hours. She and Mom called and called, but I never answered. That solitude was delicious.

Under the Rosebush

I am in love with the bracing memory of
Sunlight beaming through bare canes
Of the itinerate climbing rose
Under which I hid from the world.
No one discovered my pathway,
Maneuvering, first right, then left,
Gingerly, through the thorny mine field,
Thus to bask in solitude and air perfumed
By the fragrance of the blossoms.
The latest litter of kittens served as muses,
Scampering through the protective,
Large canes…Their antics
Vital reflections of my blithe childhood,
While my mother stood on the porch
And called and called my name.
Even now, in the midst of a frenzied day,
I can recall the peace and warmth of my secret place,
Conjuring memories, regenerate and reviving,
For, I am ever in love with the memory of sunbeams.

Time has a way of entwining sisters. Later we would be Maids/Matrons of Honor in one another's weddings. She is a wonderful aunt to my girls and her son is very special to me.

Her pathway has been different from mine, leading her into unique fields of service. Her work with Hispanic peoples, Hospice and abused women is amazing. She is especially sensitive to the needs of others. The elderly seem drawn to her and I am always impressed with the things she can get done for people.

When my husband died unexpectedly, she was a Hospice grief counselor. God was certainly timely with that, wasn't He? I don't know what I would have done without her. So many times she has come to help keep my home going when I was recuperating from some surgery or other malady.

She is the one in the family who organizes and often initiates plans for handling different crises. Our family would be crippled without her.

NEXT TO LAST

The brother that I spent the most time with was the cotton-headed, next to the last to be born. When my mother left to go to the hospital for his birth, my sister put in an order for a green baby brother (green was her favorite color). He was named Robert Walter Riley and given the nickname of Barry. Go figure the correlation in name and nickname. He was to keep the humor alive in the family. He is rather dark skinned as are most of us. However, his eyes are strikingly different. They remind me of turquoise, cat-eye marbles. His hair stood up straight on the top of his head, so we called him Dennis the Menace. Trouble was his middle name. His earliest trick related to his precocious coordination. He walked at 7 months, at 10 months he used the broom handle to unlock the screen door and run down the street to the Franklin's creek where we would find him just sitting in the water. He always had a pair of shoes drying on low in the oven, the little toes drew back as they dried. It's a wonder he did not have deformed feet. It did not matter what type of punishment he received for his daily wanderlust, he repeated the escapade often for many months.

I took him everywhere with me. He rode my hip until he was 3 or 4 years of age. We spent all day in the summers at the local pool. I tired quickly of spending much time in the baby pool, so I knew I had to do something. I wanted to be in the deep end with my friends. But, he did not know how to swim. My plan was to teach him to swim by putting him on the low diving board and telling him to "jump." On the day of his swimming lesson, he jumped as instructed. I can still see him way down next to the bottom, (I was scared thinking of what I had done) but he bobbed to the surface and dog paddled to the edge. He could not get enough of the deep end after that. I would not advise this method of teaching aquatic skills to anyone else, but it worked. To this day…he still listens to what I say. At least I think he does.

Barry was fascinated with heavy earth moving equipment and insisted on my reading to him several times a day, the book *Mike Mulligan and His Steam Shovel.* By his late teens, his obsession had not abated. When he graduated he was hired as a "Mike Mulligan" and has done this type of work ever since, and he has been quite successful.

Barry has the sweetest nature of all of the Riley children; I think we will keep him.

THE BABY

The last Riley sibling was twelve years younger than me. He was born with a shank of dark hair and a loud cry. The thing I remember most about him was that he had the nickname of "Boo Boo." I always wondered if he got that because he was not planned. Anyway we called him, "Kevin Scott Riley Boo Boo."

He was bright and loads of fun. He loved Johnny Cash's music and *"Car 54, Where Are You."* He would sit on the porch steps and mime the dialog from that TV show. He also toddled around singing, "I Fell Into A Burning Ring of Fire," coming from a 3 year old, it was quite hilarious and remarkable at the same time.

By the time he was in kindergarten, I was in high school and dating heavily. He never failed to embarrass me when I brought a date in the house. One incident involved his pet hamster, Nibbles. Kevin had just gotten his bath and been dressed in his pjays. He ran into the living room where I was and sat on the couch beside me. He had Nibbles in his hand and was letting him tunnel through his pajamas. Suddenly, he jumped and screamed, "Nibbles bit my penis." That was one bit of news I didn't want shared. I ran to the other end of the house and pleaded with my mother to make him leave the living room. It was wasted effort.

When I brought my future husband for his first encounter with the family, Kevin jumped into his lap and demanded to know, "Are you going to marry my sister?" I wanted to crawl under the floor; we had just started dating.

It seems that the role of the baby in the family is to keep things in an uproar and all the members humble. He sure didn't neglect those responsibilities, did he?

THE GANG

By the time I reached high school, the core of my social life shifted to include a group of girls that came to be known as the Gang. It consisted of Smitty, me and other girls, Linda P, Liz D, Pam C and Marlene J with others drifting in and out. We got ourselves into and out of many adventures mostly involving boys. Any week's foray might have a different leader. The election would depend on who could arrange to get the family car on a Saturday night. Once settled we were off and headed to Raleigh. Sometimes we had nothing better to do than cruise the Boulevard or the NC State campus. We were wildly flirtatious and vocal about it too.

One episode found us at a lake party, where after a while the girls were dragged shrieking and screaming toward the water. I did not get dunked; I was too tall for the guys to manhandle. I don't know how the others explained the baptism to their parents. The only good thing was it washed the smoke smell out of the clothes and hair. (We engaged in the only illicit activity we knew which was to smoke cigarettes.) It caused us to have to drive with the windows down even if it was 15 degrees outside in order to prevent smoking up the car. How stupid was that?

We often dropped into the YWCA in Raleigh for their Friday night dances. During the early 60s dancing often involved little touching and much gyrating, sometimes face to face, sometimes presenting your back to your partner. There was a young man named Robert who became a nuisance to us, monopolizing our dances. The gang decided to teach him a lesson albeit a cruel one. The scheme we cooked up was as follows: One of us would accept his invitation to dance… the others would hide behind a door leading into the room, and wait for the moment during the dance when our victim would turn and face the other direction. Then, we would all hide behind the door and watch his reaction when he turned back around and no one was there…he would be left dancing alone. It worked…we nearly fell down the stairs to the parking lot in spasms of laughter. It was a cruel joke, but still makes me chuckle to recall the look of utter confusion on that boy's face.

Another scenario this time involved just me and Smitty. We went on a beach trip with our church youth. We had no money…well, just a couple of dollars. We really did not need any money if we had stayed with the group, but that's for the boring ones, not us. Smitty and I decided to see just how many dates we could make for the same night. So, all day we flirted and arranged to meet different boys at the pavilion at the same time that night. Between us, we arranged for 15 different young men to arrive simultaneously. Meanwhile, we got dolled up and hid nearby to witness the travesty. It was hilarious. After all had arrived and sufficiently amused us by swiveling their heads as they watched and waited….we ran down the beach to a luau we had heard was going to take place. We didn't intend to be cruel; we thought it was just a big practical joke.

Of course, the times were so innocent then and we were not thinking of anyone's feelings, but our own. In my opinion innocence and compassion cannot co-exist. We had yet to know the real hurts that life would inevitably inflict. Such a stunt served to assuage our egos which were always in need of shoring up. Here is a poem to which most young women can relate.

Girl in the Mirror

She looked at herself in the mirror;
Apparently, it had never been clearer.
Her mouth too wide, her teeth not straight
Beauty was something she could not create.
Her curls were an endless daily dread;
Relentless fuzz hovering over her head.
She had no style, not even a clue;
<u>Seventeen</u>? She just would not do.
Her picture'd never be on that page;
It'd definitely be a pitiful display.
Her clothes were all wrong;
In truth, she'd never belong.
Too fat and certainly too tall;
Not one redeeming asset at all.

Time, it seemed, passed into the years
The girl, now woman, rejected her fears.
The girl in the mirror forgot her despair;
Forgot about the image she had left there.
Her world expanded, had even changed;
Her problems once simple were now exchanged.
Years now had passed, old pictures reclaimed,
Memories stored within the old frames.
She dusted them off and looked askew
Was this the person she thought she knew?
The girl she remembered was not pictured there;
But, one who was beautiful, lovely, and fair.
It took all the years of living and learning,
To find that the image she always been yearning,
Was hidden by her hypercritical eyes,
And the mirror created by society's lies.

©April Bolejack

FIRST JOB

My senior year in high school I landed a job at one of the local television stations, WRAL in Raleigh, NC. I was hired to assist Bette Elliott as a production assistant for her television show and as a general production clerk for the Sales Department. My job was to do whatever I was told. It wasn't long before I was writing advertising and cooking for Bette's show which featured various guests, cooking segments, etc. Ironically, Bette could not cook, so I often made the recipe and she took the credit. I loved the job because there were always deadlines and excitement involved with live TV.

I hadn't been there long when walking through the upstairs production booths, I saw a couple of good looking guys in the studio below. I was in a soundproof booth so I could not hear them nor could they hear me. One guy was on a 15-20 foot ladder adjusting the lights in the studio; the other guy was pushing him from light to light. This is before such things were computerized. Suddenly, as if he were possessed with a demon, the second guy began racing around the studio with the first guy holding on for dear life. I could read his lips, "Stop this thing! I mean it; Stop it!" The air had filled his London Fog jacket and I could not help but laugh. Even with that soundless separation, I could tell that he was a keeper.

About a week later, I was introduced to this young man. He was strikingly handsome with black hair and green eyes. I thought he was drop dead gorgeous. It turned out that he was working there and attending NCSU at the same time. He was a junior in the School of Engineering. His name was Garland Bolejack; he would be my husband. It was against company policy for employees to date, but we began to meet off campus in Pullen Park just down the road for lunch. I was pinned to another guy at the University of Utah, so I would not go on an official date with Garland until I had broken up with the Utah boyfriend. Therefore, I would let him take me to lunch only. Don't know why that seemed okay, but it seemed noble at the time. I remember the first lunch with the handsome studio hand was right after I had begun to wear braces. We ordered pizza. When we were leaving the restaurant GB told me that I had a piece of pepperoni stuck in my teeth. I was mortified and thought I would never see him again. But the next day we went out for lunch again. Now, that was a sign of something; I'm not sure just what.

When I finally agreed to go on our first regular date, it snowed. Down South, more than 5 flakes of snow initiates a run on the grocery stores for bread, milk, etc. Ten flakes and life is forced into a freeze frame. Dad said that I could not go out with this new boyfriend because of the weather. I was devastated. A compromise allowed for GB and his three roommates to come to the house for sledding. I lined up three members of the Gang and off we went. By the way, none of the guys had any gloves or any boots, so we used Dad's socks for mittens and bread bags for boots. We had a great time, coming back to the house for hot chocolate and banana bread. The guys stayed until 4:00 AM. I never thought I would get by with someone staying that late. Mom and Dad must have been exhausted.

In addition to meeting my husband, I met many celebrities as part of my job. Nobel Prize winner, Pearl Buck, came to the station as well as other authors, though I do not remember all their names. I do remember the singers, such as, Paul Revere and the Raiders, Tom Jones, The Monkees, Peter and Gordon and others. I remember that Gordon Mills, Tom Jones' manager, invited me up to Tom Jones' hotel room for tea. Mr. Mills was a very handsome man himself, but GB said I shouldn't go for there would be no tea. Darn it! I thought it would be super cool to go, but I took his advice I guess I'll never know what might have happened that day. Oh well, there went my five minutes of fame!

There was always an atmosphere of impetuousness in the studio. That was the nature of live television. This birthed many jokes many of them ribald. One hilarious joke played on the weatherman was to carry out all manner of foolishness just behind the camera that was focused on him. Example: one rainy Saturday night (It was always the 11:00 news on Saturday night that was chosen for such shenanigans because there was little supervisory staff to be found at that hour.) the director punched up the camera covering the weather. A cameraman began urinating in a tin pot just under the lens of the camera. Since it could be heard, but not seen, the weatherman had to cover for the noise. His comments included the sound of "the rain" being heard in the studio. The goal of the production team was to crack the weatherman up so that he could not deliver the weather. I have to admit he was a stronger person than I because he did not stumble over a single word.

Another night, the production team vowed that that would be the night that the Sports Director would be brought to his knees. This was a blood mission because no matter what had been done earlier, this man was iconic in his stoicism. He would not break. The plan was this. Ray Reeves was the voice of the Duke Blue Devils and he had taped his sports segment earlier in order to host an awards banquet for the Duke team. The producer was to tell Ray as he was exiting the studio, "Mr.

Reeve, you must come back and deliver your segment live for the tape you recorded is no good." Ray turned without a word and headed into the studio where the news was airing live. As he settled into his set, the director punched up the camera so that its red light would indicate Ray was on the air. Next the news anchorman said, "Now, Ladies and Gentlemen, here is that bald headed son of a gun Ray Reeve with the sports." Ray could not speak; he turned practically purple and just made some subhuman grunting noises. It was priceless and we all fell apart laughing. He was never the same after that… a broken man, but it made him human.

I eventually had to leave the station in order for GB to keep his job. His position was far more important than mine since he needed it to get through school. He graduated in May 1966 and we married the very next week.

EARLY MARRIAGE

Garland and I married in June of 1966. We delayed our honeymoon because the getaway car,1957 Chevy, was still in the shop. Spaghetti was served for our wedding night feast attended by my family, all seven of them. How romantic!!!. When we finally took off around midnight, we still had three hours to get to our hotel. Upon arrival we were completely exhausted. The next morning, not satisfied with the engine sounds of the car, we decided to switch cars with my new in-laws. They lived only about an hour away. Another foretaste of glory divine was the fact that as we finally hit the road to our rental cottage in Gatlinburg,Tenn. I realized I had left my purse. We had to return to get it. I had all the money…he had just graduated from NC State and literally had none. Finally, we got to our destination; unfortunately, our car smelled rather sulfurous. We ran over a skunk on one of the mountain roads. It was so pungent a smell that it made my eyes water. We trailed that scent the entire week. By the way, there is no such thing as being nose blind to a scent. Such relief is the pure imagination of some wishful thinking advertising executive

Later that week, we decided to go fishing at Douglas Dam. We had so little money that I had to cook on our honeymoon. Anyway, I made a picnic of fried chicken, potato salad, etc. As my beloved fixed his plate, he made a fatal error. I hope you will learn from his mistake. "This potato salad is not like my mother's." Those words scorched my heart. I whirled around, picked up the serving bowl of potato salad, threw it lock, stock and salad into the trash can and said, "Well, get your Mama to make you some." He just stood there in shock, wondering what he had done wrong. By the time we parted company in this world…he was a wise man in the use of verbiage. Life is a stern taskmaster sometimes.

After the honeymoon, we headed to Connecticut to begin our married life…both of us green as gourds experientially. We arrived in the Hartford area with nothing but a backseat full of wedding presents. Neither of us had any experience with the tangle of interstate highways that flow in and out of that capital city. Some of the routes were toll roads. After a car repair bill in Silver Springs, Maryland, we had almost nothing left until his first paycheck. In Hartford, we inadvertently headed in the wrong direction and ended up crossing the Charter Oak Bridge spanning the Connecticut

River. It had a toll of $1.00. We paid and turned around to pay again crossing back over the river to catch the correct route. Somehow, we ended up repeating the same mistake three more times. The fourth time, I leaned across and spoke to the toll taker, "Please, we are lost and cannot afford to keep paying this toll. Can we please just turn around and try again?" His cold response, "That will be $1.00." That man needed some lessons in Southern hospitality in my opinion.

The seedy motel where we landed after the toll debacle was not even on the right road. Garland had to do some creative driving just to get to work. After an interminable length of time in rental purgatory, it was quite a relief to find a furnished house. We were down to our last plug nickel, but GB got an advance on his first paycheck and we were living high. At least we thought so.

Still, weekends were lonesome times, but we became skilled at finding things to fill the time. We spent many Saturdays and Sundays fishing, sightseeing, skiing and ice skating. We tried it all. Everything was so different and interesting. We still missed home though. We missed the South, so when we flew back from visiting home, we often carried a country ham with us along with a quart or two of Duke's Mayonnaise and other items necessary for living.

The North had its advantages also. Sometimes we would catch the train and travel two hours into NYC. We had, ironically, one of our most infamous fights in the Statue of Liberty. GB wanted to walk up the stairs into the head, and I did not wish to traverse those myriad steps with some stranger's butt in my face and mine positioned likewise. I refused to go. GB went anyway. I lost him in the process and looked everywhere for him, finally I saw him just as he was about to board the ferry. He was going to leave me there on that island!!!! I screamed his name from the base of the statue. He looked back and I shouted, "You'd better not leave me here!" As usual, he started to laugh. That always made me madder. Now, that I look back on it…it was very humorous, but not so funny at the time. I can only imagine what the onlookers were thinking. Don't misunderstand; we had many wonderful times together and even when we were "fussing," it was hard not to laugh. I mean we did some crazy things. We were both young and dumb… a dangerous combination.

CHRISSY, OUR FIRST BORN

In 1966, Garland and I married and moved to the Hartford area of Connecticut. Three years later, we started our family. April Christine was born on March 29, 1969. She was a tall, lanky baby from the start. I remember that she literally filled the hospital bassinet.

Today, almost forty years later, she is just shy of six feet with very long legs and arms and a total charmer with looks to match. I know that she has some mannerisms like her mother, but she looks a great deal like her dad, and her gentle spirit has given her the ability to work well with people. She is a real leader; someone who can entice others to do what they really don't want to do, and like it anyway.

Her father was exactly the same way. They share the same work ethic. I think the motto is: Whatever it takes. She certainly has a full plate today with the management of her part of a chemical plant, elderly grandparents, and a mother who has a debilitating disease. I so admire her patience and even-toned personality.

She developed her work ethic on our farm. We farmed sheep because we knew the girls could handle them better than cattle. I have a vivid picture in my mind of Chris running through the pasture with her hair streaming behind her while chasing lambs and/or ewes. She could pick one up and throw it for shearing or medicating. She could throw hay and back a tractor better than her Dad. She has always been tenacious, maybe even a little stubborn.

In her first five years, we spent almost every moment together. I taught her songs, about nature, and she soaked it all in. We trekked through the creeks and talked about pollution. Once she wrote a letter to the editor of the local newspaper complaining about an industrial polluter. I was proud of her then and I am more than proud of her now. When her Dad died in 1996, she was my rock. She helped settle the estate and was instrumental in helping me through the shock and depression that followed.

In her public school days, she wrote with great talent. I haven't witnessed much evidence of that since engineering school, but I wouldn't be surprised if that talent re-emerged at some time. Perhaps she will carry on the family tradition of writing…I don't know. I hope either she or her sister will carry the baton for the next generation

Now, she is the mother of my first two grandchildren, Zachary and Madison. I could not love anyone more than my grandchildren. There are three, but the other one belongs to her sister, Danielle.

I believe that grandchildren are God's great do-over. All that we believed was so important, and maybe it was, is overshadowed by the compulsion to just LOVE. I wouldn't have missed this for the world. She is a fabulous mother, married to a man who is a fabulous father. I thank God for both of them.

Sacred Song

The years have passed long since
You skipped the pastures green,
And paused to study reverently
Abundant nature, simple and free.
I heard you as you sang your song
Child-like, soft and fair,
A pastoral tune of inspiration;
A jubilant strain I long to hear.
Pray sit you down my child
And with your pen do write
The sacred words that draw the light
From a simple song sung right.
Writing down the past it seems
Makes all the years draw clear
And so parades for all again
What was happy and so dear.
The past is such a holy thing
Guardian of our dreams,
And never can we see as clearly
As the child who once ran free.

DANI

At the old age of 25 and 29 respectively, we had our last baby. She was to provide many moments of joy in our lives. At birth she was exquisitely beautiful. Her black hair looked as if it were tipped with blonde, very thick and so long that the nurses were overheard telling one another to go and see the baby "with the wig."

A better baby could not be found, for she would go through the terrible twos and threes dragging her blankie and tugging on my clothes offering to go to bed when she was tired. Now, that's every mother's dream.

She was cuddly and very attached to me. I took her everywhere and she was most malleable. Her yellow blankie was her constant companion, and it was truly a security to her.

I remember that she did not like her picture taken, so almost every picture we have of her prior to school age, she has tears in her eyes.

She loved her older sister and when Chris began kindergarten, Dani missed her sister so that she invented an entire imaginary family for company…the Weekson family. If she was being scolded for something, she blamed it on them. "Lisa Weekson did it; I didn't do it." That was her truly imaginative reply.

She was two when we moved to the farm and she developed into a true country girl. There were no dolls, etc. in her toy box; she wanted tractors and Big Wheels. She played *with cars, trucks, and tractors in the sandbox.*

Later when we raised sheep, she was always too little to get a good throw hold on one, but she worked side by side with her dad and sister to dock tails, give vaccinations, and worming medications.

We bought her a horse and she developed into a fearless rider. Her sister was more reserved, but Dani galloped full speed ahead all over the farm. She loved it.

As she grew, she developed a natural buoyancy and I loved to hear her laugh. She did have one characteristic that got her into trouble with her dad, her shrill scream. It was ear piercing. Her daughter, Avery, has inherited that shriek and I have laughingly said, "It is poetic justice."

In her teens, her striking looks led her to enter the *Seventeen Magazine's* cover model contests, which she won for the area. We did not pursue this any further since we hoped for college later.

She did graduate from UNC Wilmington with a degree in Environmental Science and Marine Biology. Later she got her Master's Degree in elementary education. That was quite a feat. Dani has always had a native, kind of logical intellect. She instinctively knows how to handle people and zeros in on what the issues are and what is important and what is not. That has served her well, especially when she was teaching first grade. Her serendipitous characteristics drew her students to her and they loved her. Danielle is still the delight of my days, and I can count on her to keep her eye on the prize. She is my levity in the bread of life.

When she left us, she took much joy and laughter with her, but she has given me my third grandchild who is just a cookie cutter version of her mom, scream and all! I am so thankful to know this little one.

So Grown Up

Come on over here,
And tell me what you did today.
Climb up on my lap,
And chat of every wonder
That caught your eye.

And, when you tire of
Being such a big girl,
Will you press your little
Head against my breast
And let me rock you
gently as I used to do?

FARM LIVING

After we moved back to North Carolina, we decided we could improve our girls' childhood by buying a farm. When we moved to the farm, we took GB's beekeeping hobby with us. One of the outbuildings was perfect for his honey extracting equipment. We bought an automated device that used centrifugal force to sling the honey out into a barrel from which we could fill jars. Some may label this a luxury, but it saved our marriage. Garland had used the kitchen to bottle his first harvest of honey. I never did get all the beeswax off that floor. We sold that house with all the wax on it that we could not get up.

We had up to 60 hives of bees at any given time. The girls hated working out there because there were bees flying around…left over from the taking off of the frames. They were afraid of them. I didn't blame them.

I had a healthy respect for those minions of pain myself. Sometimes when GB would work the hives… he had the beekeeper's "Bwana" suit and hat for protection; we did not…the bees could get awfully disturbed and would then be looking for revenge. That's the scenario that led to my unfortunate temporary disfigurement. Once Garland was doing something to the hives after the spring honey flow. The bees, without much to do, became quite agitated. The telephone rang; it was for him, and I headed in his direction to call him to the phone. While I was still several hundred feet away… BAM! One flew right up my nose, stinging me in the process. Now that's a tender part of the anatomy and it hurt more than any other sting I have ever had. I cussed a blue streak and threatened all sorts of vile retribution on those sadists. In fact, the part of the garden where the attack took place failed to thrive that year after my scorching outburst. I don't know if I was responsible, but it helped to assign blame and I did it. My lip swelled bigger than a Hollywood madam's after a collagen appointment. I looked like a freak. There have not been many times that I have been angrier than I was that day. GB scampered around trying to make it better, but I could swear I saw just a slight tremble and upturn in the corners of his mouth. That man loved living on the ragged edge. Okay, it wasn't a mortal injury, but sure felt as if it might be, and truth be told…his life and the life of those bees…were all in danger. My eyes watered from that for quite a while and they weren't just tears of rage.

A STUDENT AGAIN

After the children were school age, I decided to fulfill my destiny. I enrolled in college. Although this chapter appears to be a distinct shift in focus, it shows that the skills I have manipulating language have served me well in and out of the classroom. Growing up in a five-child family, compels one to be quick with a verbal retort. I found that humor is a most valuable tool in the classroom discipline arsenal.

I have found that in many situations, humor has the power to defuse potential confrontations with a student and having the humorous attitude allowed me to laugh at myself and in that way helped create the atmosphere I wanted in my classroom.

For example, one of the most humorous incidents that I recall was rather serious in its nature. A very troubled young man was distracted during a writing assignment. I passed by his desk three times and each time he was reading a rock music magazine. At every pass, I whispered for him to put the magazine under his desk and begin the assignment. On the third request, He shot up out of his seat and threw the magazine on the floor. "Stupid witch," he yelled as he left the room. I turned to the class, now wide eyed and struck dumb and remarked. "It's okay…I'll be right back," "I've been called a witch before, but the stupid really did hurt my feelings," then I headed to the office for backup.

After a few years, I became known for unusual comments issued in response to classroom situations that cropped up frequently.

These were labeled Bolejackisms or the verb form was to be Bolejacked. Once, these were collected by several of my students and presented to me in a scrapbook at the end of the year. Here are a few:

* If you don't quit that, I'm going to tap dance on your head with my stilettos on.
* Stop talking or you will find your tongue stapled to the desk.

* Quit doing _____or I'm going to have to hit you so hard when you wake up all your clothes will be out of style.
* Have you enjoyed being _____years old? That's good 'cause you might not make it another year.
* You had better get your act in gear or on graduation night, you'll be part of the audience.
* I don't care if you've never done it this way. Change is inevitable. If man did not change he'd still be crouched around a fire eating raw meat."

Although these sound rather Stooge-like in their threats, teenagers are often similar in their quips to one another. They knew I loved them and was laughing with them. Such quips often defused and amused.

More often than not, the student provoking the situation had no idea how amusing it was which only made it more hilarious? We had a classroom that was filled with laughter. Often the teacher next door complained that her students were jealous because it sounded as if we were having so much fun. Learning is supposed to be fun! I believe it and we worked just as hard at learning as we did in having fun. There are always standout students who capture your heart and your giggle box.

One student who has forever burned herself into my memory, is a student I'll refer to as B J. B J was from a rather deprived background, both financially and socially. She, as many other students in our rural setting, had not been exposed to many social situations. One reason is that our schools served a rural population with long bus routes. For this reason, students who were eighteen or older could take a test and if they passed, drive a bus. (They can no longer do this.)

BJ passed the bus driver licensing test. This was a real source of money for her, I imagine. BJ was a large black girl, and she was one tough cookie...not likely to take much off her student/passengers. One morning in the lounge, I heard the assistant principal say that there had been some complaints filed on one of our busses (no one knew the bus number) whose passengers were throwing bottles out the windows as they drove down the road. The store owner/caller complained, "We appreciate the business, but we DO wish they would bring the bottles back." This was in the days when glass soda bottles were recycled and the deposit refunded when they were returned. It appeared upon investigation that BJ's daily regime was to leave the school, shuttle her passengers to the local convenience store, where they would all pile off the bus, purchase their snacks, load back up, consume their purchases, then dispense of the evidence as BJ drove the assigned route. Of course, the bus had travelled a ways before the students began to launch their ammunition. That's why it took a while to discover the driver of that missile launcher. BJ loved driving that bus...but she seemed to be unaware that when she drove it home, it was to remain parked. Busses were for school activities, not for personal use. This lead to another fine mess. A large cheese wagon (school bus) was reportedly seen driving all over town on weekends. An investigation ensued since the gas to operate the bus was enormous... Now the "cheese wagon" as the students referred to it, which could seat approximately 60 students, had been reported as carrying one or no passengers. It turned out that BJ was transporting her mother to work. (One person) and then going to visit her boyfriend in the county jail. I find the mental image of her mother jostling around in the back of the bus with no one else and then BJ pulling into the parking lot of the county prison in that big orange cheese wagon most humorous.

Eventually BJ lost her bus which was, I am sure, a substantial financial blow to her family. The reports indicated the kids sure had some rackety times on her bus, and you never knew where that bus would show up.

Today, education is unlike anything I experienced in the Cary Schools. We never know what will happen during the course of a day. There may be the threat of violence from a student or someone out in the community. Teachers are expected to serve as "parents, medical community, counselors, social workers, and more roles too numerous to mention. I mean what member of my generation ever heard of a "lockdown?"

Lockdown

Today, we read Macbeth,
Gaining privy to
His plans to murder Banquo,
Observed the development of Huck's
Conscience; while a man brought a gun
To the school and we had lockdown.

We studied the thesis statement,
And the diminishing Lady Macbeth.
Later, we pressed ourselves
into a corner,trying to be quiet
in our fear because
a man came with a gun
And today we had lockdown.

We studied slavery and how
Man is indifferent to the
Suffering of his fellow man,
Realizing that we have lost
Our human sensitivity,
So, today we had lockdown.

In the news we heard about
A school shooting in a
Neighboring state and how the
teachers did all
they could to save students
While today we had lockdown.

Only the teachers were here
To comfort the terrorized,
Offering sacrificial love because
There was a man and a gun
And we sought our only
hope in lockdown.

THE WRITER

I really cannot tell you when I began to think of myself as a writer, but I do know that it took a while to take myself seriously. At first, all that came out was humor. I wrote a parody of Ann Landers in the high school paper and parodies of many cartoon characters and love songs.

Later, as an adult, I wrote "special occasion" poems, which were usually humorous. It took studying and growing to love the poetry of the master poets to develop my own style. I'm not sure that I have a style, but I suspect that it is closest to Miss Emily Dickinson's writings of love, nature, loss, and connections with the Divine.

At first, when I began writing in earnest, my poetry was maudlin. It seemed that for me to write, it had to be a release on a "pressure valve" of sorrow.

Now, my inspiration comes from every area of my life. The tiniest flowers and insects can send me for paper and pen. Just the joy of being alive is an inspiration.

This one thing I know…my life is richer for the gift of being able to express myself in a poem or even in prose. I believe that most psychiatrists and counselors could be out of practice if people spent some time in writing/reflecting each day. That is the gist of how I present writing to students. It is a part of being human. Like it or not, we communicate with one another through this medium. Those of us who can manipulate words and do it beautifully and memorably have the power to change the world.

It is an awesome responsibility….I do not take it lightly. Here are a couple of poems that express this probably better than I have done here.

Poet's Brush

The poet's brush is dipped in lexicon.
The paints describe her native vista round;
And all that she perchance may look upon,
Or whatever her eyes may see, be sounds.
With measured syllables, melodic voice,
She paints first sky and then the ancient tree.
"God's grandeur" piercing first, her heart's best choice;
N'er more perfection could her eye there see.
Her record breathing life into the sphere,
And so scripts the holy conception found.
Illuminating words to charm the ear,
Well-set syllables and sensuous sound.
If words her art, no higher to aspire,
A gift of God no power could e'er acquire.

©April Bolejack

My Unspoken Message

Here's my unspoken message to the world…
All of those who did not understand me:
The words and thoughts are every one contained
In the images I paint, you see.

Some poems I write are born through timeless scripts
Whose design gives construct and conceit?
Presented to reader on silver leaf,
Improvident feast meant for dining replete.

A poem is not a poem, you see
If written to please the critical eye,
Unless each chosen word means two or three…
Without it contains the self-soul reply.

Poetry is not just words strung carefree;
It is art that is divinely inspired,
Given with heavenly account required,
Bestowed on the poet, never acquired.

©April Bolejack

THIS AND THAT

During my lifetime, I have tried to look on the humorous side of things, and there have been occasions that have been more than just humorous. let me tell you about a few. When I was doing my teaching internship, I was assigned to a 7th grade literature class. We were doing research in the library on topics related to the historic setting of "Rip Van Winkle." One boy had George III, the ruling English king during the story's setting, for his research topic. He called me over to his table and announced, "I can't find this man in the encyclopedia; he ain't got no last name." I had never thought about it, but he was right. It was not a situation I had counted on having to explain.

Another time I assigned research topics during a unit on early Greek civilizations. We were reading *Oedipus, the King*. One young man and a partner had the poet and author, Homer, assigned to them. They were to find information with which to share with the class. In a few days, these two young men stood to take their turn and began sharing a visual report, complete with illustrations, about the American artist, Winslow Homer. I asked them why they got headed in that direction and again they said, "That other guy had no last name so we thought you meant this one." There is a period gap of about 4000 years there, I explained between gulps of swallowed giggles.

Later during another occasion, a young man was absent from my class for about a week. The kids, when queried, reported, "His girlfriend is having a baby." Upon his return, he presented a note from an obstetrics group on their printed prescription pad that read (in the student's handwriting) "Please excuse Edward. He has a broke toe." I just laid my head on the desk and laughed. I couldn't help it. It was so ridiculous. Edward was still staring poker faced when I was able to compose myself. "Just go sit down," I said. There was nothing to do but mark his absence unexcused. School notes are full of humor. One reported that her son had the die rear. And another said that her daughter had "vottomed" all day. I wish I had the memory to recall all of them, but there is not space or time enough.

The students are sometimes full of practical jokes. When I was called to the office once, I returned to find that the kids had removed all the furniture from the room and hidden it behind the backdoor that led to the library. Imagine my reaction to that. Of course, I played some jokes on them myself. Another call to the office led me to get on the intercom to my room and announce, "This is God speaking. No talking while Mrs. B is out of the room." As I returned I turned the corner to my hall and the quarterback of the football team was running toward me saying, "Mrs. B, Mrs. B, I've had a religious experience. God spoke to me while you were gone." That young man got the best one on me that day.

I think during my career that I enjoyed my students and I hope they enjoyed me and learned much also.

THE LAST WORD

After this intense perusal of my life's events, I can truthfully say that things are so different from the years of my youth. Who could have dreamed the population explosion that took place in Cary in the 1960s? Who could have imagined that I would get lost in my own hometown some day? But I have.

I am now more than middle aged and I am glad to have come this far on my journey. I envision those who come after me reading and laughing as they read this epistle. I hope these memories have provided both humor and wisdom for those who take the time to read them.

ACKNOWLEDGEMENTS

Thanks to Gail Tattersfield for planting the idea and Jon Goldstein for insisting that I publish this for my friends and family.

I appreciate all those who tasted the previews and found them palatable.